THE BIG BOOK OF CARD TRICKS FOR KIDS

INTRODUCTION

WELCOME TO THE WORLD OF MAGIC!

Hello, dear friend! Welcome you to a wonderful world of amazement! I'm so excited to take you on an exciting journey down the rabbit hole of MAGIC!

I have a question for you. Have you ever heard the saying **"those who do not believe in magic will never find it"**? No? It was famously said by a very wise man called Roald Dahl. You might not know this man personally, but I'm sure you must have read or heard about his books, like Charlie and the Chocolate Factory and Fantastic Mr. Fox.

Yes, these are truly magical worlds that all of us know so well. We can almost step right into them and imagine that we are really there! The interesting thing is that Mr. Dahl probably never performed a magic trick, but he was a magician with his stories. Just like you and me, he understood that magic is something to believe in, or one might never find it.

Your belief in magic is the reason why you are reading this book, and I'm thrilled that you are here. You will not only find magic here, but you'll learn how to share it with others, spreading happiness and wonder to everyone around you.

This is the greatest gift you can ever give to anyone!

I've got something even MORE exciting to share with you... The Big Book of Card Tricks for Kids is only the first book in an entire series of magic books. After this book, we have book two, and then book 3, which teaches you everything you need to know about MAGIC!

In book two, you'll discover all sorts of amazing tricks that work all by themselves (these are called 'self-working magic tricks'), and in book three you'll discover loads of amazing tricks that you can do with common everyday household items. The series of three books contain everything you need to become an incredible magician!

So, are you ready?
We have a long and exciting journey ahead of us!

And what better way to introduce you to magic than to start with the most amazing card tricks that all magicians love to perform? So, I have decided to start the series with The Big Book of Card Tricks for Kids.

Buckle up and let's go!

This book is divided into three parts and each of them contains 10 tricks. So in total, you have 30 tricks to study, practice, and perform. First things first, though. You need to know a few important secrets before you get started. Let's start with... '**the Magician's code**'.

THE MAGICIAN'S CODE

The magician's code is an important set of secret rules that all magicians know very well. Yes, you are now a magician in training, so it's time you understood the magician's code.

You must remember this code always, and never forget them. If you do, you could ruin the magic, and all the fun will disappear... So, even though it may be tempting to ignore these rules, you'd better read them well and remember them always. Got it? Ok, listen close.

1) Never reveal your magic secrets

After you amaze your audience, people will most likely pester you for your secrets, but you mustn't tell anyone, not even your best friend or family members.

Can you remember the first magic trick you ever saw? Wasn't it great? Did you wonder, "how did he do that?" If you found out the truth you'd stop wondering and the magic would disappear. So, if you can keep the secret hidden, the audience be kept in a constant state of wonder.

If someone nags you for the secret, just shrug your shoulders and say, "It was magic!" Don't spoil your magic and their fun. When you refuse to share your secrets, you will have joined the club of all the professional magicians who protect these secrets. They are for you and I only.

2) Practice, practice, practice!

When you learn a new trick, you probably won't get it right the first time. This is completely normal. If doing magic was that easy then it wouldn't be so amazing any more. Instead, you will need to practice, and practice... and practice some more. Until you can do it without dropping the cards all over the place. Until it looks completely flawless. And until you can do it every single time with your eyes closed. Practice will also help you to speed up. If you do the trick too slowly, everyone will see how it's done.

So, how do you get it right? Practice, practice, and then practice some more! And enjoy practicing! That's half the fun – the learning process. And then you can look back and see just how far you've come, plus it's such an amazing feeling when you can thrill your audience with your new magic trick!

3) Do not repeat the same trick twice

Sometimes, after you have thrilled the audience, they will shout, “Do it again!” But you mustn't do it again... Why? Because someone in the audience will be watching you very carefully.

They know how the trick ends, but they'll be waiting to see it again, so they can try to catch you and discover the secret. Instead, move straight onto the next trick, so the audience doesn't get a chance to discover the secret.

4) Do not announce the expected result at the beginning

It's very tempting to tell the audience what you're about to do. For example, "I will make this card disappear!" or "a ball will magically appear in the cup". When people know what to expect, they'll lose interest and instead just be waiting for the end to happen. They'll also be thinking about how you do the trick.

Instead, I'll teach you how to use 'misdirection' to direct your audience's attention to something else. So when you finish the trick, the audience will be completely surprised. They'll never have expected it to happen that way – and they'll be amazed!

5) Move quickly from one trick to the next once you've finished.

You don't want to give the audience any time to think about how the trick was done. They might figure it out if they have lots of time to think about it. Instead, keep their attention by amazing them with yet another awesome trick!

Now that I've revealed to you the hidden secrets of the magician's code, here are a few tips on how to put on the BEST magic show possible.

HOW TO PUT ON AN AMAZING MAGIC SHOW!

Learn how to do at least a of couple tricks REALLY well (at least 4 or 5). You should be able to do them with your eyes closed (not literally!)

When you put on a show, pretend that you're someone else. Magicians are also actors. You can create a completely new character, be a different person. It all adds to the sense of illusion.

Perform for an audience as often as you can. The best way to become less nervous and to improve as fast possible is to perform in front of people as much as you can. A great tip is to carry a deck of cards with you in your pocket wherever you go, and when there's some time to kill, whip them out and ask "can I show you a quick magic trick?"

Don't be nervous. This is easier said than done, but a nervous magician makes mistakes very easily, forgets what to say, and loses confidence in the audience. For this reason, it's really important to practice in the mirror first to become great at presenting. Another tip is to imagine your audience NAKED – if anything it'll give you a good laugh!!!

Practice facial expressions in front of a mirror. As I said in the last point, confidence is everything, and there's nothing that shows confidence more than through facial good expressions. Don't just practice smiling, but also practice looking shocked, amazed, confused, and more... You'll need these expressions for the tricks later on. You'll use them to build a story, to build suspense, to misdirect the audience's attention, and to keep the audience engrossed in a trick.

Practice talking or joking with the audience. Some magicians don't say a word, some perform to music, and some even sing... but what I recommend in this book is that you become very good at talking and joking with the audience. This puts both of you at ease. You can even adjust the tricks to their interests and behavior as you improve.

A trick without a story is just a cheap thrill, but by talking and joking you can build up an entire performance around a single trick. For example, instead of a card just disappearing, you can start talking about how in quantum physics particles can appear and disappear at the same time, and that you've learnt to control it, or tell a story about why you want to change the suit to something else, so you can win at poker... Being able to tie the tricks into a believable story is an amazing skill to have that will MASSIVELY improve the quality of your magic shows, and amaze your audience even more.

Since this book is all about card tricks, you need to own at least one deck of cards. If you don't have one at home, ask your parents to buy one for you. But it's not enough to just own a deck of cards. To be a good magician, you'll need card knowledge and a good memory. So, lets learn a few skills that you can do with a deck of cards, especially fanning them out and shuffling.

FANNING OUT CARDS

Put your left hand out with your palm facing upwards and your fingers spread a little. Place the cards on the palm of your left hand, so that the top edge of the cards is between your thumb and your index finger. Move your fingers, so that the pinky is out of the way, and your ring finger is resting on the bottom, right-hand corner of the deck.

Let your thumb rest on the top of the cards touching the ring finger (or as close as you can get to the ring finger). Use the index finger of the right hand to fan the cards out. Don't hang on to the cards, if you do, they will not fan out. A little secret tip: before you fan the cards, spread them out a bit.

card during a trick. Whenever you use, it always looks very impressive, so be sure to add it into your performances.

SHUFFLING CARDS

Here are a few different types of shuffling that you should know, and practice often. You can do them at any point during a trick, or before/after the trick. It'll maintain the flow of your performance and keep the audience hooked.

RIFFLE SHUFFLE

This is a tricky shuffle to begin with, but it looks very impressive when it is done correctly. Depending upon how well you shuffle, the cards will be very mixed up. In fact, a perfect riffle shuffle should have the cards alternating perfectly! You'll see what I mean...

● Split the deck in half and hold both piles longways between your thumb and middle fingers (with both hands). Make sure your thumbs are not sticking out too much over the edge of the cards.

● Using the table for support, let your thumbs slowly release the cards as you push down on each pile using your index fingers. The edges of both piles should overlap.

● You can assemble the pack again by pushing all the cards back together. When you get good at that, end it off with a bridge shuffle. This is when you bend the merged mile of card the opposite way and the whole pile will slide into place.

OVERHAND SHUFFLE

This is the easiest and most common shuffle.

- Hold the deck in your left hand, the top corner should be resting by your index and middle finger with the thumb resting on the back of the pack. (If you're left-handed, put the deck in your right hand.)

- Hold the deck longways in your left hand, the top corner should be resting by your index and middle finger with the thumb resting on the back of the pack. (If you're left-handed, put the deck in your right hand.)

- With your right hand, grab most of the cards with your middle finger resting on the top, and your thumb resting on the bottom. Lift out a bunch of cards and slide them back into the pile again at random.

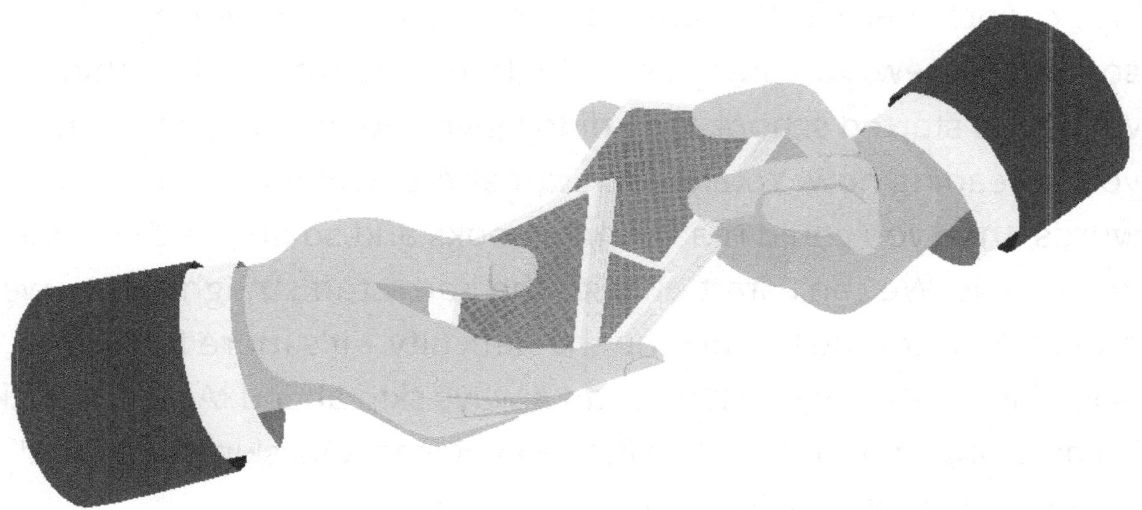

HINDU SHUFFLE

This is a useful shuffle to use if you want the bottom card to stay at the bottom. This shuffle will come in very handy later.

- Hold the cards in your hand, like you did for the overhand shuffle.

- Instead of taking out bunches of cards from the side, you will slide them out longways. So with your other hand, pinch a bunch of cards from the middle of the deck and then place them on top

- Repeat this action quickly. It will look like you are shuffling up the cards very well, but actually the bottom card stays the same.

PART ONE: EASY-PEASY

This chapter deals with some easy tricks. When you learn something new, you always start with the easy things. Just think when you started school, they didn't give you books like the ones you're reading now. You had to start at the beginning and learn words, then you could read simple books and so on. It's the same with magic. We can't start off with the hard stuff straight away, we must take our time to build up the difficulty – it's more fun this way! If it's TOO easy then you can always skip ahead. Also, if a trick is confusing or you don't like it, then you can also skip ahead and choose one that you like better.

1. QUEENS TO THE TOP

QUICK INTRO: You'll need a pack of cards and some quick preparation for this trick. When I say "quick" preparation, I mean it. Here it is:

PREP ONE: Before you begin, take four random cards from the deck, and place the four queens UNDER them.

PREP TWO: Keep these eight cards in your hand.

STEP ONE: Show the bottom of the pile in your hand, and say something like, "These cards are the Queens, and they're heading to their castles." You can show your audience the queens but be careful to hide the 4 random cards behind the last queen.

STEP TWO: Now put your little pile of eight cards face down on top of the deck, so the queens are now buried under the top 4 cards.

STEP THREE: Take the first card and insert it somewhere in the pack and say, "This is the first Queen, and she's headed to Windsor Castle."

STEP FOUR: Do the same with the next three cards mentioning other castles or places.

STEP FIVE: After all the random cards have been placed in the pack, tell your audience that the queens are returning for a Royal Ball!

STEP SIX: Now, here comes the show! Cover the cards with a scarf if you want, then tap the table forcefully with your hands near the deck. Your audience will be wowed when the first four cards you take from the deck are the four Queens.

LAST WORD: Viola! Bow out or quickly move to another trick. Remember to never give your audience the chance to think too much about your trick. Easy, right? Lets try another!

2. THE RED QUEEN AND TWO BLACK ACES

QUICK INTRO: You will not need a full pack of cards for this trick. You will only need the queen of hearts and the two black aces.

STEP ONE: Lay the three cards face up on the table with the queen of hearts between the black aces. The ace of spades should be the first card and the ace of clubs the third card.

STEP TWO: Ask for a helper from the audience. Let's call the helper Deborah. Assuming no one offers to help, then you must choose someone. I always prefer that someone offers to help because you can't be blamed for planting a helper in the audience.

STEP THREE: Look away or turn around so you can't see, and ask Deborah to choose a card. She must not touch or move the card that she chooses. She must just look at it. Tell her to show it to the audience.

STEP FOUR: Whilst you are still looking away, ask Deborah to change the places of the other two cards. In other words, she should swap them around.

STEP FIVE:.After she has done that, ask her to turn all of the cards over, so you can only see the back of the cards. It's now time to face the audience again.

STEP SIX: Ask Deborah to move the cards around on the table. Keep your eyes fixed on the middle card.

STEP SEVEN: Ask her to put the cards next to one another like before, still face down, and you're still watching the card that was in the middle.

STEP EIGHT: Turn over the card that you were watching.

LAST WORD: Now here comes the fun part. If you turn over the queen of hearts, you can say, "The card you chose was the queen of hearts." And the audience will be so surprised. If you turn over the ace of spades, the card they chose would have been the ace of clubs. If you turn over the ace of clubs... surprise! Deborah chose the ace of spades.

3. THE RED AND BLACK TRICK

QUICK INTRO: You need a full pack of cards for this trick. This one needs a bit of preparation.

PREP ONE: Separate the cards into a black stack and a red stack.

PREP TWO: Put the black stack on top of the red stack.

STEP ONE: Now, ask for a helper from the audience. Let's call the person Kathy.

STEP TWO: Fan out the cards face down on the table, and ask Kathy to choose a card, and show it to the audience.

STEP THREE: Tell Kathy to lremenber the card she chose.

STEP FOUR: Pick up the stack, and fan them in the opposite way. Tell Kathy to put the card back more or less in the same place as before. The card she chose will now be a different color from the cards around it.

STEP FIVE: Pick up the stack and fan it towards you, so you can see the faces. You can then take the odd card out and show it to Kathy and the audience.

LAST WORD: Once your preparation for this trick is good, you will always put on a good show. I must say this again. Your show will look real only if you act the magician.

4. SLEIGHT OF HAND

QUICK INTRO: Do you know what "sleight of hand" is? I have named this trick after the move because you will need it to pull off the show. When your audience is distracted, you do a quick move with your hands. This trick requires a very simple sleight of hand.

STEP ONE: Shuffle your cards and have someone from the audience select a card. Let's name that person Stacey. She can show it to the audience if she likes, and then put it face down on the table.

STEP TWO: Whilst the audience was looking at the card, glance at the bottom card in the deck you are holding, and remember it. Now ask Stacey to divide the pack into two piles. They don't have to be equal size packs. They must place the packs side-by-side on the table.

STEP THREE: Tell them to put their card on top of the first pile, and then put the second pile on top (so now the bottom card is sat right next to their card in the middle of the deck.

STEP FOUR: Lightly shuffle the pack but be very careful. You don't want to disturb their card or the one you peeped at. There is a very high chance these two cards will stay together if you just do a light shuffle (but not always).

STEP FIVE: Then, deal the cards one-by-one face side up, pausing sometimes as if you're trying to get a message from the cards.

STEP SIX: When you see the card that you peeped at, you know that the next one is their card.

5. THE MAGIC CARD

QUICK INTRO: To start this trick, you need a pack of cards. You must be able to spell the numbers from ace to ten, the words jack, queen, king, and the four suits: spades, clubs, diamonds, and hearts. You must also be able to spell the word magic.

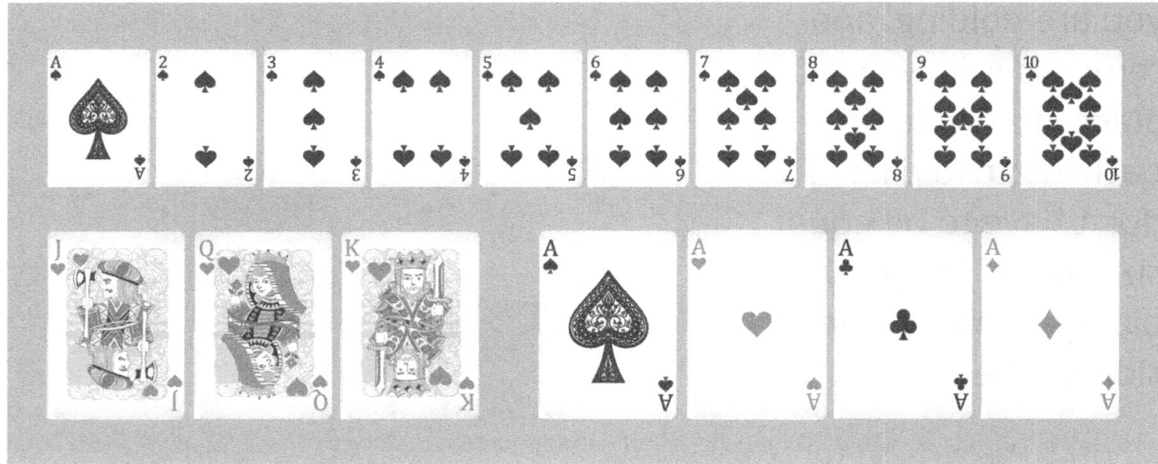

STEP ONE: Ask for someone from the audience to come and help you. Let's assume the person's name was Matthew.

STEP TWO: Shuffle the cards and ask Matthew to shuffle them as well.

STEP THREE: Count out nine cards, and put the rest of the deck to one side – we won't be using the rest of the cards. Place the nine cards face down in three piles. Each pile must have three cards.

STEP FOUR: Ask Matthew to choose a pile and look at the bottom card. This is your magic card.

STEP FIVE: Hold the pile face down and collect the other two piles under the magic card pile. It's very important that this pile is on top

STEP SIX:. Now comes the spelling part! Let's say that the magic card was the nine of hearts, you need to spell that out. As you say "N" place the top card on the table. "I," place the next card on top of the first one. Carry on until you have spelled the whole word.

STEP SEVEN: Place the pile on the table under the pile in your hand.

STEP EIGHT: Spell the word "OF," and place those two cards under the pile in your hand.

STEP NINE: Spell the word "HEARTS," and place those five cards under the pile in your hand.

STEP TEN: Then, finally, spell the word "MAGIC." The last card will be the magic card.

LAST WORD: Some magicians like to call this trick the spelling bee. What a neat way to enjoy spelling!

6. READING THE MIND OF YOUR HELPER

QUICK INTRO: You need a full pack of cards for this one. But, it needs a bit of preparation.

PREP ONE: There are 52 cards in a deck. You want to halve the pack, so there are 26 cards in each pile.

PREP TWO: Place one pile on top of the other, so that it's slightly askew or not fully together. The audience must not be able to see the break, but you need to see it. Now you're ready to face the audience.

STEP ONE: Ask for a helper from the audience. Let's call the person Sam.

STEP TWO: Pretend to cut the pack just anywhere, but you know where the break is! Remember, this is your secret and no one must know. Otherwise, you do not have a show.

7. WHAT'S THE BOTTOM CARD?

QUICK INTRO: All you need for the trick is a pack of cards. You do not need to prepare for it. Just go right into the trick.

STEP ONE: Ask for a helper from the audience. Let's call the person Joey.

STEP TWO: Ask Joey to check the deck to see if it's a normal deck.

STEP THREE: Now, get Joey to shuffle the deck. (If he doesn't want to, ask him to watch you as you do the shuffling the deck.

STEP FOUR: Take a quick look at the bottom card before holding the pile in your left hand.

STEP FIVE: Ask Joey to tell you when to stop as you use your right index finger to slide the cards towards you.

STEP SIX: When Joey says "stop," take the cards that you have separated as well as the card at the bottom. No one must see you sliding that bottom card out. It will now be at the bottom of the new pile. Slip the new pile underneath the main pile. Yes, you're right. The bottom card is still the same one!

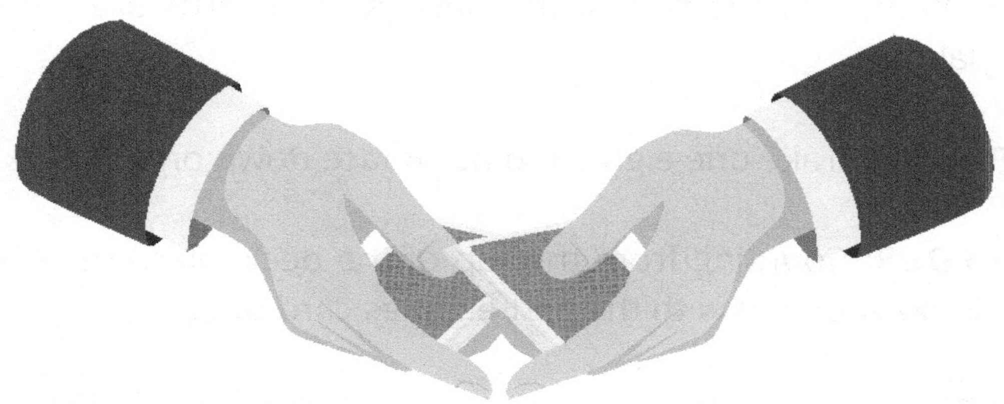

LAST WORD: Step Two is important because the audience sometimes guess that you are using a fake deck. So, if the trick does not need preparation, then you can always ask your helper to check it. Step Five might look like the hard part. Don't worry you will get it as long as you practice until you are very good at it. It's called a "sleight-of-hand trick" because your hands must work quickly to confuse the audience. You can do this a few times. Talk to the audience or tell some jokes. Yes, talking to them will distract them from watching your fingers. Make a show of sliding the bottom card out. Show the audience, and make sure they know that you can't see it. Say, "I think this is the..." (and name the bottom card). Viola! You have done it.

8. EiGHTS ARE COOL

QUICK INTRO: You need a pack of cards for trick. But, you need to prepare the pack before the show.

PREP ONE: Take all the eights (hearts, diamonds, spades, clubs) from the deck.

PREP TWO: Hold the rest of the deck, so the cards are facing your palm.

PREP THREE: Take one eight, and put it face down on the deck.

PREP FOUR: Counting from the top of the deck, place the second eight in position ten with the first eight as card one.

PREP FIVE: Flip the deck over and have it facing up, count seven cards down, and place the final two eights in spots eight and nine.

PREP SIX: Flip the deck back over and have it face down again. And now for the trick!

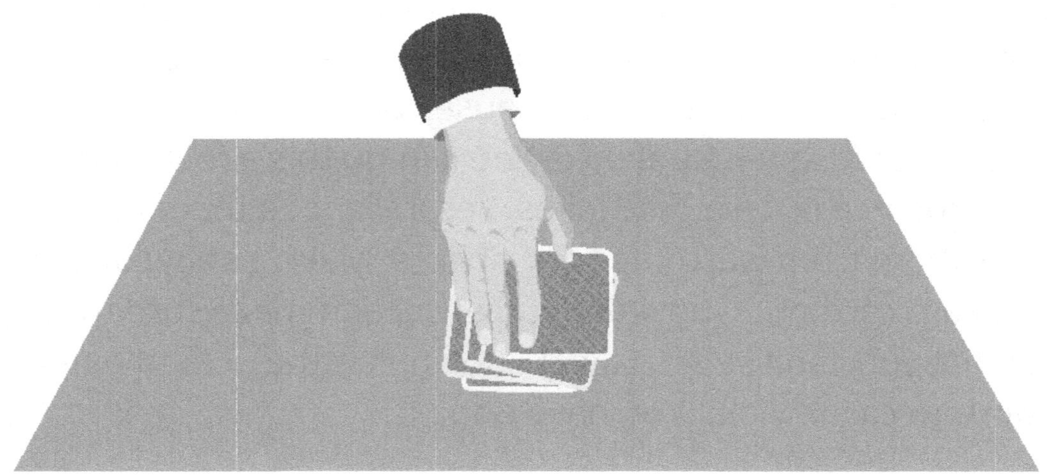

STEP ONE: Start fanning the cards out from one hand to the other. While doing this, count to ten cards silently because this is where you put an eight.

STEP TWO: Take that card out of the pack, put it face down on the table and tell your audience, "This card is going to help me in this trick."

STEP THREE: Now, move the cards from one hand to the other, and from the bottom, count the cards in your head as you go.

STEP FOUR: When you have counted out nine cards, say to your audience, "I'm getting bored. Tell me to stop!"

STEP FIVE: At this stage, divide the cards into two decks. The eights will be towards the bottom of one deck and at the top of the other.

STEP SIX: Place the bottom deck on your right and the top deck on your left.

STEP SEVEN: Flip over the top card on your left, and place it face-up next to your "prediction card." This should be an eight if you counted correctly.

STEP EIGHT: Explain to the audience that this indicates the deck is instructing you to take eight cards from the bottom of the pile on the right. Explain that because it's an even number you must start at the bottom.

STEP NINE: Pick up the pile on the right and count out a fresh pile of eight cards from the bottom of the deck, keeping the cards face down.

STEP TEN: Show the bottom card (which should be an eight).

STEP ELEVEN: Turn over the top card of the pile, which should be an eight as well, and show your "prediction card," which should be the first eight.

LAST WORD: And there you have it. Another one in the bag!

9. SLIP ON, JUMP ON

QUICK INTRO: You will need two packs of cards. This needs a bit of preparation before you go on stage.

PREP ONE: Remove the five of spades and the ten of diamonds from both decks.

PREP TWO: Place one deck on the table as you will not need them until the end of the trick.

PREP THREE: Hold the other deck in your hand and place a five of spades on top and the other five of spades at the bottom face down. Do the same with the ten of diamonds. Now, you are set!

STEP THREE: Place the two cards back on the deck face down and wave your hand over the deck while saying the words, "If I have the power to make cards jump0 then you owe me an air fist bump

STEP FOUR: Tell the audience bump. "that the cards have traveled to the bottom of the deck. Do not let anyone touch the cards.

STEP ONE: Walk up to your audience]you owe me an air fist and say the words, "If I have the power bump." to make cards jump, then you owe me an air fist

STEP TWO: Turn over the first two cards on the top of the deck and show the audience.

STEP FIVE: Turn the deck over and reveal the two bottom cards. Remember you placed the duplicate cards there before the show.

STEP SIX: Now, say the words, "I have the power to make cards jump, now you owe me an air fist bump," and let them give you air fist bumps, and bow out.

LAST WORD: Okay, that was a good one. You and I know making cards jump is not possible. You did this because of your preparation. But, I'm pretty sure that you will fool your friends and family, especially the kids. Many of them will think you have super powers. It feels good, doesn't it?

10. TWO STACKS

QUICK INTRO: You need a full deck or cards and a bit of preparation for the trick.

PREP ONE: Separate the cards into suits before performing your trick.

PREP TWO: Put the hearts and clubs in one pile and the diamonds and spades in another.

PREP THREE: Combine the two heaps, but slightly twist the top pile, so you can see where one pile stops and another begins but the audience can't.

STEP ONE: Ask for a helper from the audience. Let's call the helper Wesley.

STEP TWO: Split the cards into two piles, and place both next to each other on the table.

STEPTHREE: Ask Wesley which pile he wants to choose.

STEP FOUR: Tell him to shuffle his pile after which he is to choose a card.

STEP FIVE: While he is deciding on the card to choose, take the other pile from the table.

STEP SIX: Ask him to place his card anywhere in the pile after making his choice.

STEP SEVEN: Lift the cards, so they face you and fan them out.

STEP EIGHT: The card whose suit doesn't fit in with the other two suits is his card.

STEP NINE: Show it off to the audience and take a bow.

PART TWO: MEDIUM SQUEEZY

Phew! That was quite a lot, wasn't it? One part down, two to go. Magic is so fun and being able to perform it is even better! If you haven't mastered the tricks yet, there is plenty of time. Take your time and go back to the easy tricks if you still must master them. If you feel ready, jump on in, and follow the instructions for the tricks in this chapter. The stakes are getting high now. You can do it! It's going to be great! You'll be able to show off your newest skills with confidence, amazing all your friends and family.

You don't have to worry about messing up because you know you have what it takes. That's right. We practice confidence here; it's one of our special ingredients when cooking up a magical storm. Haven't found your confidence yet? Relax, it's coming. Doing something impressive like performing a magic trick in front of a crowd, getting it right, and being able to entertain your friends... now that's a confidence booster! So before continuing, why not go back a few steps. Find one card trick in the previous chapter and try to master it. Then find a small audience and perform for them. Build confidence for the other tricks, and then move into this new chapter. Go on, give it a go!

11. ELEVEN CARDS

QUICK INTRO: For this trick, you will need a regular deck of cards. Also, you need to prepare for it ahead of your show. It's a simple prep. So, no need to worry.

PREP ONE: Remove one ace, one jack, and one of each card numbers 2–10. It doesn't matter which suit they are, but you should now have eleven cards.

PREP TWO: Starting from the middle of the table and going right, lay the cards down in the following order: 6, 5, 4, 3, 2, Ace, Jack, 10, 9, 8, 7. You can put the cards face up or face down, face down gives a bit more mystery. Now to the steps!

STEP ONE: Ask for a helper from among the audience. Let's call the person Nate.

STEP THREE: Tell Nate to move one card at a time from right to left (starting with the first card you lay down—the six). Before he starts, turn your back, and ask him to count how many cards he moved. Tell him he can move none or as many as 10 cards.

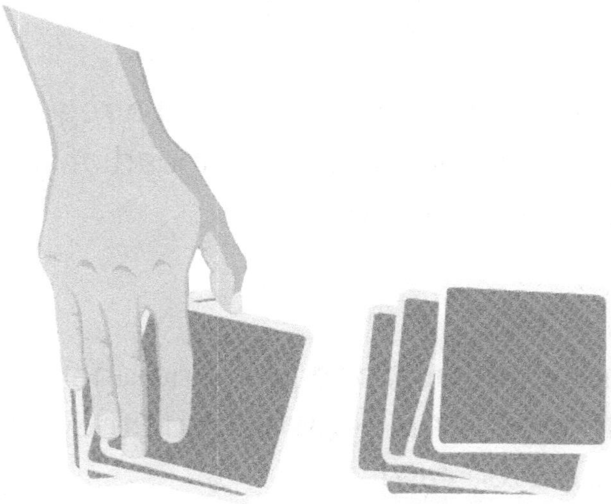

STEP FOUR: When he says he's finished, turn back and stare at the cards, silently counting seven cards in from the left. If the cards are face up, just tell him how many cards he moved. If the cards are face down, flip the 7th card, and tell him that's how many he moved.

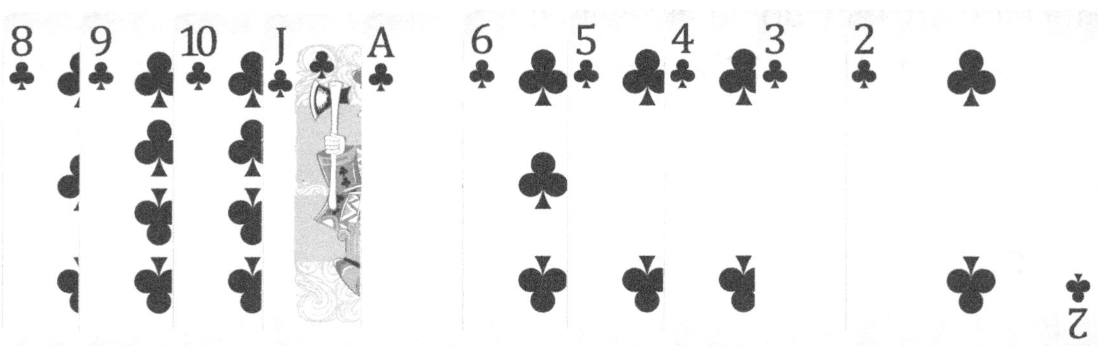

LAST WORD: This trick always works. Let me show you an example. If they moved five cards, the new order would be: 8, 9, 10, Jack, Ace, 6, 5, 4, 3, 2. The 7th card is 5! If they do not move any cards, the seventh card will be the Jack. That will tell you that no cards have been moved.

12. COPY ME

QUICK INTRO: You will need two complete decks without jokers. Try to use decks that have a different back.

STEP ONE: Allow an audience member to choose any one of the decks. Let's call this person Smith. Instruct him to follow your lead.

STEP TWO: Shuffle the cards and then cut them making sure you see the bottom card. Let's pretend that it's the Queen of Hearts.

STEP THREE: Ask another member of the audience to come up to the stage. Let's call her Loretta. Give your deck of cards to them to check that it's not a trick deck.

STEP FOUR: Ask them to cut the deck and place the cards on the table with the bottom pile on the left and the top pile on the right.

STEP FIVE: Ask them to take the top card from the pile on the left, remember this card, and then place it on top of the other pile without showing you.

STEP SIX: Now, instruct them to take the pile on the left and put it on top of the pile on the right. While it appears that their cards are being jumbled, in fact, their card will be placed next to the one you remembered (Queen of Hearts).

STEP SEVEN: You're performing the same task as they are, but you don't need to remember any cards other than the Queen of Hearts.

STEP EIGHT: Take your deck of cards back and ask them to use the other pack to find their card. When they find it, they must place it face down on the table.

STEP NINE: Start flipping each card from your deck while you pretend to search for his card. However, you're looking for the Queen of Hearts. And their card will be the next card. Place it face down.

STEP TEN: Count to three and ask them to show their card, and when you flip the cards over, you'll have a perfect match!

13. THE QUEEN SEES EVERYTHING

QUICK INTRO: This one is a bit long. While reading through the steps, make a few notes to help you remember everything in a way that you will understand. Your magic might seem to be getting harder! Truth is: Go through this very slowly and practice it a lot before doing it in front of an audience.

STEP ONE: Shuffle a deck of cards yourself or have an audience member do it for you. I always prefer that you call on someone from the audience. Let's call that person Kennedy.

STEP TWO: Ask Kennedy which queen should assist you with the trick. Let's say they chose the Queen of Clubs

STEP THREE: Spread the cards out, so you can see the face of the cards. Take the queen of clubs (or whichever queen they picked) and set it aside.

STEP FOUR: While the cards are spread out, look at the card that will be on top when you close the pack and remember it.

STEP FIVE: Close the fan of cards and put the cards face down on the table. The card you were looking at is now on top.

STEP SIX: Put the queen card face down on the table and cover it with your scarf. Tell the audience this is so the queen can't see the next part.

STEP SEVEN: Ask Kennedy to pick up about a third of the pack and put it on the right side of the pack. Then, take about a third again and put it on the right side again. Your card will be at the top of the middle pack.

STEP EIGHT: Ask him to point to one of the piles of cards.

STEP NINE: Okay, this is a bit hard now. Remember your pile is the middle one.

> **a.** If he points to the middle pile, say, "Good, We will keep that one."
>
> **b.** If he points to either of the other piles, say, "Okay, we get rid of this one" and set it aside.
>
> **c.** You must now force him to choose the pile you want. Ask him to put his index finger on each pile, count to three, and then he must remove his finger from one of the piles.
>
> **d.** If he lifts his finger from what was in the middle pile, say, "Okay, so this is the one you want."
>
> **e.** If he lifts his finger from the other pile, say, "Okie dokie. We need to take this pile away."

STEP TEN: You now have the pile you want. Turn away from the cards and ask Kennedy to pick up the top card to see which card it is.

STEP ELEVEN: With your back still turned, ask him to shuffle the pack in any way he wants. When he's done, he can tap you on your shoulder.

STEP TWELVE: Ask Kennedy to do one last thing. He must spread the cards on the table.

STEP THIRTEEN: Now say, “Right queen, please show me what you want me to do.” Slowly wave the queen over the cards on the table a few times.

STEP FOURTEEN: Bring the card up, so you can see the face, and pretend you're listening. Then say, “Okay, I know what you want me
to do.”

STEP FIFETEEN: Turn to Kennedy and say, “The queen says your card was the...” They will be amazed when you say their card.

LAST WORD: This trick is quite hard. Go through the instructions as many times as you need to. It's okay to not get it the first few times.

14. THE MIGHTY CARD FLIP

QUICK INTRO: With this trick, you will need a full pack of cards.

STEP ONE: Get a helper from the audience to shuffle your pack of cards. Let's call the helper Frankie.

STEP TWO: Fan the cards out but make sure that the pack of cards is face down while doing this.

STEP THREE: Ask Frankie to take a card and turn around to show the audience. Everyone in the audience including Frankie must remember what the card was.

STEP FOUR: Talk about anything interesting (maybe a piece of joke) to distract the audience. As you do this, turn the pack around to see the faces. While they're distracted, take the first card and flip it face down.

STEP FIVE: Ask them to put their card, face down, anywhere in the pack. You will now have two cards that face a different way. Make sure you know where the helper's card is.

STEP SIX: Swap the cards from hand to hand, making sure that at the end all the cards are face down except the bottom one and Frankie's.

STEP SEVEN: Cut the deck below the Frankie's card. Set the top pack aside.

STEP EIGHT: Pick up the top card from the bottom pile and flip it over and ask if this was Frankie's card. Act confused when he says "No."

STEP NINE: Now, say to him, "Then it must be in the other pile."

STEP TEN: Pick up the other pile, turn them face up, and fan out. Act surprised that one card is the wrong way. Ask Frankie to take the card out.

STEP ELEVEN: Ask them if that's their card. And there you have it

LAST WORD: Step Four is very important. You are all set once you have flipped down the first card. Frankie would think all the cards are still the way they were. The rest of the trick is acting from Step eight to Step ten.

15. THE MAGIC FOUR

QUICK INTRO: The Number 4 is not always seems as a magic number unlike 3, 7 and 9. You just might add number 4 to the list of magic whole numbers after this trick. So, get a full pack of cards.

STEP ONE: Select a helper from the audience and ask them to shuffle the pack of cards. Let's call the helper Sandra. Tell her to cut the pack if she wishes.

STEP TWO: Fan the cards face up on the table to show it's an ordinary pack but make note of the 4th card from the top. Let us pretend for now that it is the two of hearts.

STEP THREE: Gather the cards together, making sure you don't put the 4th card anywhere else.

STEP FOUR: Ask Sandra to cut the pack and place the cards in two piles on the table. Make sure you know which pile has your 4th card.

STEP FIVE: Pick up the bottom pile and peel the cards off one at a time, look at the face of each card as you discard it. When you get to the 4th card, stare at it, and then say "This card has a message. I need to find the two of hearts. It's the 4th card in the other pile."

STEP SIX: Pick up the other pile and fan out the top four cards. Ask Sandra to take the 4th card. Amazement all around!

16. I'LL SEE WHAT YOU SEE

QUICK INTRO: You need a deck of cards for this trick. Also, you need a good memory. By now, I am sure you have seen that a magician needs a good memory. I know you have one. So, we are good to go.

STEP ONE: Ask for a helper from the audience. Let's call the person Amanda.

STEP TWO: Ask Amanda to spread the cards out in a fan with the faces showing. This is to show that the pack is not a trick pack.

STEP THREE: Make sure you remember what the 1st card (the top card) is.

STEP FOUR: Collect the cards together and place them face down on the table.

STEP FIVE: Ask Amanda to cut the deck and place the two piles next to each other on the table.

STEP SIX: Take the bottom pile and place them face up on the top pile.

STEP SEVEN: Tell Amanda to cut the pack again and place the bottom pile on the top pile face up.

STEP EIGHT: Slide the cards off the pack until you come to the first face-down card.

STEP NINE: Show the audience the top card and pretend you're looking hard at the back of the card. Look hard at the audience, and say, "I can see the card that you see. It's the..." (whatever card you noted at the beginning)

17. SPELL YOUR CARD

QUICK INTRO: You will need an ordinary deck of cards for this trick. You must also make sure that you can spell all the numbers, the special cards, and the four suits.

STEP ONE: Ask for someone from the audience to help you. Let's call the person Brad.

STEP TWO: He is to pick a card from the pack and show it to the audience. It'd be good that you turn your back for this part.

STEP THREE: Take a quick look at the bottom card while your back is turned.

STEP FOUR: Ask Brad to place his card on top of the pack. Then he can cut the pack and put the bottom pile on the top pile. Your memorized card will now be on top of the Brad's card.

STEP FIVE: Fan the cards out. Find your card. Look at the card on the right of your card, and this is the one you must spell out. Start with your card and work to the left spelling out the Brad's card to yourself. When you finish spelling the card's name say, "I am going to cut the pack again."

STEP SIX: Cut the pack and discard. Pick up the pack carefully.

STEP SEVEN: Ask Brad to tell you what card they picked.

STEP EIGHT: Deal the cards one by one while spelling out loud the letters of their card. When you get to the last letter, flip the next card over, and it should be the helper's card.

LAST WORD: Deal the cards one by one while spelling out loud the letters of their card. When you get to the last letter, flip the next card over, and it should be the helper's card.

18. REVERSED CARD

QUICK INTRO: This trick is almost the same as the beginning of The Mighty Card Flip, but the end is different.

STEP ONE: Ask for a helper from the audience. Let's call the person Patricia. While she is coming up to help you, turn the bottom card around.

STEP TWO Fan the cards on the table but make sure Patricia cannot see the bottom card, so you let the last few cards clump together. Ask her to choose a card.

STEP THREE: Collect the remaining cards together and flip the whole deck, so your back-to-front card is now at the top.

STEP FOUR: Ask Patricia to slip her card into the pack. Your card and hers will be facing the wrong way.

STEP FIVE: Tell the audience something like "I'm going to find the card and flip it, so it faces the wrong way... and I am going to do it behind my back."

STEP SIX: Take the pack behind your back and flip the last card, so that it's now the correct way.

STEP SEVEN: Hand the pack to Patricia and say, "Find the back-to-front card, and tell me if I turned the right card around."

LAST WORD: She will be amazed! Make sure you follow the instructions for this one more closely. It's not that difficult, but it can trick you. Well done if you have it right.

19. THE FRISBEE CARD

QUICK INTRO: This trick is done with one card, and there's a bit of preparation. One thing you must make sure of is that your audience is not too close.

PREP ONE: Tape a piece of thread to the back of a playing card. Try to get it as close to the middle of the card as possible.

PREP TWO: Tie the other end of the thread to something on your costume like a button or belt. You may have to use a longer or shorter thread. Maybe start with a long thread, and then you can cut off as much as you need. A good length is when you can stretch your arm out and the card dangles about a ruler-length down.

STEP 0NE: Make sure that the thread lies between your first and second fingers. Hold the card and throw it as if it was a frisbee.

STEP TWO: Move your hand around, and it will look as if the card is following your hand. At the end, you can show the audience the front of your card.

20. SWITCHEROO

QUICK INTRO: This is quite a hard trick, so it will need a lot of practice. When you first start, you will probably find that the cards fall all over the place. I know mine did. So, here's a little trick you can use when you start.

PREP ONE: Get two rubber bands.

PREP TWO: Cut the pack and put one rubber band around the bottom half (we'll call this half "pack B" for bottom) and one rubber band around the top half (we'll call this half "pack T" for top). This trick allows you to cut the pack using only one hand. It's great once you have it down pat. Your audience will love it.

STEP ONE: Take a whole deck of cards in your hand. Divide the deck in half using your thumb and let the bottom half (B) rest in your palm. With your fingers and thumb, grasp the second pile (T).

STEP TWO: Move the B pack with your middle finger, so it turns in the palm of your hand.

STEP THREE: Carry on doing this until deck B is standing on its edge. It should be away from the T deck. Let your middle finger keep pushing the lower part of deck B until there's nothing under the T pack.

STEP FOUR: Allow the T pack to fall into your palm once B is out of the way.

STEP FIVE: Then let the B pack fall on top of the T pack, and you have switched their places.

PART THREE: A LITTLE BIT TRICKY

21. PINKY FLIP

QUICK INTRO: This is just a neat trick to turn the top few cards over and then back again.

STEP ONE: Loosely hold the cards in your left hand.

STEP TWO: Let your thumb push the top two or three cards away from the pack.

STEP THREE: Let your pinky rest under those two or three cards.

STEP FOUR: You can use one or both hands to straighten the pack, but make sure your pinky stays under the two or three top cards.

STEP FIVE: Slide your thumb towards your other fingers. Your index finger should be under the top cards as well as the pinky. Your thumb and index finger will work together to separate those few cards.

STEP SIX: As your thumb slides, your index finger will guide the cards to separate and then flip the cards onto your thumb. The pinky will stay in position to separate the cards.

STEP SEVEN: Repeat to bring the cards back to their position.

LAST WORD: To pull I want you to remember the following. One: the pinky keeps the cards separate. Two: The thumb pushes the cards away from the pack. Three: The index finger guides the cards to fall over.

22. DiFFERENT BACKS

QUICK INTRO: You will need two packs of cards for this trick. It is important that the backs of the cards are different. I think it is good you use decks of a different color or a different design.

PREP ONE: Select one card from the second pack and put it at the bottom of the first pack.

STEP ONE: Ask for a helper from the audience. Let's call the person Monica.

STEP TWO: Now, you're going to be doing the Hindu shuffle. Remember, I explained it in the introduction. As you begin to shuffle, ask Monica to shout stop anytime she wishes.

STEP THREE: As soon as she shouts "stop", show the bottom card in your right hand (or left hand if you are left-handed) and say, "You have chosen this card." Now, name the card.

STEP FOUR: Put this card face up on the table and spread the other cards next to it face down.

STEP FIVE: Ask Monica to turn her card over to show the back. What a surprise! The back is different!

23. TOP DECK

QUICK INTRO: As we have been doing in most of the tricks so far, we audience participation for this one. A pack of cards is also needed.

STEP ONE: Get a helper from the audience. Let's call the person Jack.

STEP TWO: Ask Jack to examine the pack, and then shuffle it. When he gives it back to you, hold the pack, so the backs of the cards face you.

STEP THREE: Now here comes the hard part. You must fan out the 2nd, 3rd, and 4th card. The first card must be hidden behind the pack.

STEP FOUR: You now must instruct your helper to choose one of the three cards, but they mustn't say anything or touch any of the cards. You will help them by saying "Choose one (and touch it), two (and touch it), or three (touching it)"

STEP FIVE: Tell them, "Remember your card, and whether it was one, two, or three."

Hold the cards in the palm of one hand. Ask them which card they chose, one, two, or three. If they chose:

a. *One; you take the top card (remember it was the hidden card) as you count "one" and push it into the middle of the pack. Now you can show them the card they chose.*

b. *Two; take the top card as you count one and push it into the pack. Then take the second card while saying "two" and push it into the pack. Turn the third card over.*

c. *Three; do as before for the top three cards. Turn the fourth card over.*

LAST WORD: You can add as much acting as you like to make it more impressive.

24. MENTAL SHIFT

QUICK INTRO: This is a mental trick, that is, a trick of the mind. You need a deck of cards for it.

STEP ONE: Get a helper from the audience. Let's call the person Luke.

STEP TWO: Tell Luke to shuffle the cards and give the pack to you when he thinks he'd had enough.

STEP THREE: Ask him for two types of cards, just the value not the suit. If they give you a suit say, “My power is a bit off today, so let's just have the value and not the suit.”

STEP FOUR: Cover the pack with your scarf, and stare hard at it for about 15 seconds. (Do you know the trick to count seconds? One Mississippi, two Mississippi, three Mississippi, and so on.)

STEP FIVE: Then you can say, “Wow! That was hard. I hope it worked.”

STEP SIX: Your helper, Luke's job is to take the scarf away and spread the cards out on the table. When they look for the pair of numbers they chose, they will hopefully find them next to each other or close by.

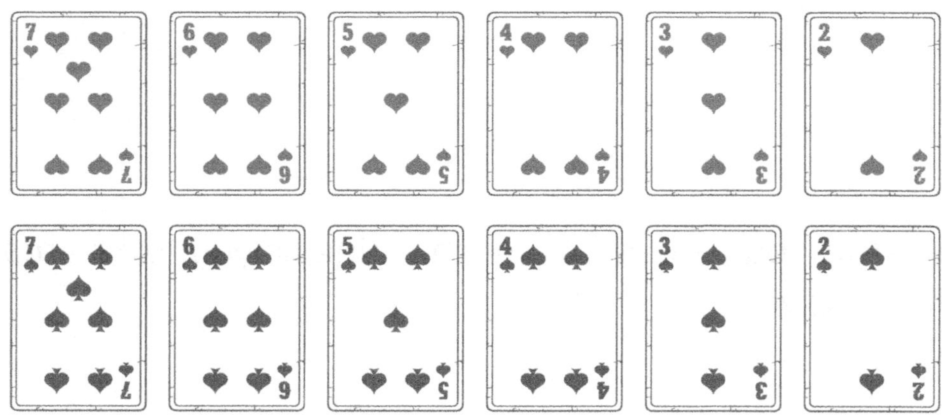

LAST WORD: This trick will work perfectly sometimes, but because it's based on something called "The Law of Probability", it may not work. I mean when your helper looks for the pair of numbers that they chose and cannot find it, the trick has not worked. But, if the trick doesn't work, you can give an excuse. You can say something like "My power is bad today. I almost made it happen, they're not too far away from each other."
Cool, isn't it?

25. I SPY WITH MY LITTLE EYE YOUR CARD

QUICK INTRO: If you like to spy on things, you are going to love this trick. You need the pack of cards for it

STEP ONE: Ask for a helper. Let's call the person Lorenzo.

STEP TWO: Tell Lorenzo to shuffle the cards. When he's done, ask him to place the pack face down on the table.

STEP THREE: Ask him to cut the pack and place the piles next to each other on the table.

STEP FOUR: Now, Lorenzo should pick a pile, take the top card, remember it, and put it back on the pile.

STEP FIVE: Pick up the other pile and look at the bottom card while you distract the audience. A short cool joke should do.

STEP SIX: Place your pile on top of the Lorenzo's pile. The card you looked at will be on top of his card.

STEP SIX: Do a cut, but make sure it doesn't go near the two cards.

STEP SEVEN: Now peel off the cards face up until you see "your" card. The next one is the Lorenzo's card.

26. A QUICK MEMORY TRICK

QUICK INTRO: You need a full deck of cards and a bit preparation for this trick.

PREP ONE: Take a secret Peek at the top card before shuffling. Let's say the card was Ace of Diamonds.

PREP TWO: Memorize the card and make sure is remains on top of the deck after shuffling.

STEP ONE: Shuffle the deck of cards and ask for a helper from the audience. Let's call the helper Beatrice.

STEP TWO: Tell Beatrice to take a group of cards from anywhere in the pack of cards. You are to collect the group from her. As you pass them back to her, count the cards in your mind. If she chose 12 cards, the selected card will be the 12th card from the pack of cards.

STEP THREE: Ask her to select a card from this group of cards and place it face down aside on the table. Make sure your head is turned for this step.

STEP FOUR: Beatrice will shuffle the remaining 12 cards from the group. Then, ask her to place it on top of the pack of card. Remember, the Ace of Hearts is on top of the card. Only you know this.

STEP FIVE: Now, you are to take a group from bottom of deck and ask Beatrice to shuffles these and place on top of the deck. Then, cut the deck.

STEP SIX: Spread the cards face up and search for Ace of Diamonds without anyone knowing. Now, count 12 to the left and the 12th card will be Beatrice's card.

27. SHUFFLE, CUT, AND LOOK

QUICK INTRO: You need a good memory for this trick like many other previous magic in this book. It also requires a lot of preparation.

PREP ONE: Arrange from a deck of cards a stack of two suits. Let's say Hearts and Spades. Mix them together.

PREP TWO: Remove the Ace of Spades and the King of Hearts from 26 cards. You will now divide the 24 cards into two piles of twelve cards each. Make sure the Hearts and Spades are well mixed.

PREP THREE: Place six cards (let's say Clubs and Diamonds) on the face of each pile.

PREP FOUR: Place the piles face down and place six cards on top of one and eight cards on the other.

PREP FIVE: Now, put the two piles together by placing either half on top of the other. With this, you have 12 Clubs and Diamond in the center of the cards.

PREP SIX: Lastly, place the Ace of Spades and the King of Hearts third and fourth from the bottom of the deck.

STEP ONE: Ask for a helper from the audience. Let's call him Dave.

STEP TWO: Ask Dave to give the pack of cards riffle shuffle. You remember this type of shuffle, right? He should do that just once.

STEP THREE: Then, tell him to cut the cards and remember the suit of the card he cut.

STEP FOUR: Now, Dave should turn the deck over (face towards him), look for the first card of the suit he cut, and remember the card.

STEP FIVE: Again, ask him to shuffle again and hand over the cards to you.

STEP SIX: Find out the color of the cards Dave cut. Ask him like, "You cut a cherry colored card, right?" or "Perhaps, it's a black Cherry". By knowing the color, you will be able to know the suit. If it is a red color the card must be the King of Hearts and if a black card, the card is the Ace of Spades. Now produce the card in your favorite way.

LAST WORD: The preparation is very important. You must get it right. Also, you must get Step Six right too. Once you can find out the color of the card that Dave memorized,

28. MONEY ON THE LINE

QUICK INTRO: You need a bit of preparation for this. Also, you need four helpers. Let's call them Helper 1, 2, 3, & 4.

PREP ONE: Take an ace and place same on top of deck and then on the bottom of the deck place the other three aces.

STEP ONE: Call for four helpers from the audience. Tell them you will show them something that they all have in common.

STEP TWO: Ask Helper 1 (male) to count down from your deck as he likes and stop. Ask him to put a penny on top of his pile.

STEP THREE: Collect the rest of the deck and ask Helper 2 to do the same but put a nickel on his pile.

STEP FOUR: Collect the rest of the deck and ask Helper 3 to do the same but put a dime on his pile.

STEP FIVE: Collect the rest of the deck and ask Helper 4 to do the same but put a quarter on his pile.

STEP SIX: Turn over each pile. You have 4 Aces as something that your helpers have in common.

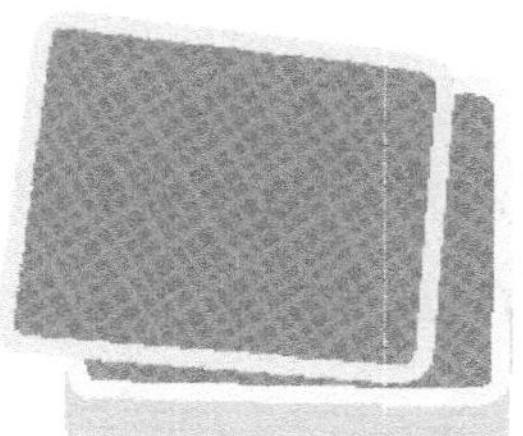

LAST WORD: The money is just to keep the helpers busy while you handle your secret. So, what is this secret? The first ace is already on top so when spectator counts his cards on the table his ace is on the bottom of his pile. Now when you take cards back and ask spectator "to place a penny on his pile" while he is locating the penny you have plenty of time to bring another ace to the top. Which you do.

This same procedure is carried out while spectators are looking for their coins to place on top of pile. You always hold the deck while they are looking for their coins which give you plenty of time to bring an ace from the bottom to the top of the deck.

29. YOU RUN THE SHOW

QUICK INTRO: In this show, you will get your helper more involved.

STEP ONE: Look for a helper. Let's name your choice Dami.

STEP TWO: She will ask you to choose a card from a deck.

STEP THREE: After doing this, you will replace the card in the deck.

STEP FOUR: Ask for a pencil and paper and write the name of a card upon the paper which you will give to Dami to hold for later identification.

STEP FIVE: Now she has to mention any number between one and twenty-six. Let's say she mentioned 17.

STEP SIX: Ask her to count 17 cards off the top of the deck and turn over the 18th card for you to see. Immediately say, "I am sorry that is not the card." The 18th card remains on top of the deck now spectator replaces her 17 cards on top of the deck and then you should say "Well, if it wasn't in the upper half of the deck maybe it will be in the lower half of the deck so give me a number between 26 and 52 cards.

STEP SEVEN: Let's suppose the Dami says "33". She counts off 33 cards into a pile and again shows you the 34th card (which remains on top of the deck). Again, say "I am sorry that is not my card."

STEP EIGHT: The 33 cards are placed back on top of the deck and you patter about it should work and then say, "17 from 33 is how many?"and Dami says "16". Count off 16 cards and look at the 17th card that remains on top of the deck and there he finds the predicted card. The paper is unfolded and there is the name of the card.

LAST WORD: Your drawing is for distraction. While Dami helps you get a pencil, you are to take a quick look at the top card of the deck. That is what you will write down on the paper. Now, the numbers between one and 26 is just reversing a number of cards. Have her look at the card on top of the deck (not at the number she selected). Now get a number in the lower half of deck between 26 and 52 and again look at the top card of deck (not the number spectator mentioned). Now subtract the lower number from the higher number and count that many cards off the deck and turn the next card over and that is the predicted card.

30. SPECTATOR'S NAME

QUICK INTRO: You need to be on top of your acting game to pull off this one. Also, you need a full deck of cards.

STEP ONE: Get a helper from the audience. Let's call the person Stevie.

STEP TWO: Ask him to remove any number of cards up to and including six cards and place same in pocket.

STEP THREE: He should then count down the same number of cards in the deck as the number of cards they removed from the deck and remember the denomination of the card at that position in the deck. In other words, if they removed four cards and placed same in their pocket, they would now look down four cards in the deck and remember the fourth card.

STEP FOUR: Take the deck for the first time and asks spectator his full name, say it is "Dami Campbell". Count the letters in the name, which in this case is twelve letters, and spell the name given. When you reach the last letter of the name, turn the card, and this is the card Dami looked at when the trick was started.

LAST WORD: The secret to this trick is simple. When you have your helper's name, which has twelve letters, reverse eleventh cards (one less than the helper's name) on top of deck by shuffling them off into the left hand one at a time. Replace these cards on top of deck and have the helper return the cards he has placed in his pocket to top of deck. Now go ahead and spell the helper's name and turn over the last letter. This will be the helper's selected card.

CONCLUSION

I hope you have enjoyed learning all these tricks as much as I have enjoyed teaching you. Most of these tricks need a helper from the audience. You can keep the same helper if there's a small audience, or you can change the helper for every trick.

Make sure your patter is perfect. So, what do I mean by patter? Patter is the things that you say to distract an audience from the important part of the trick. This can just be comments, or it can be jokes. You must practice this when you practice your tricks.

Remember the saying “practice makes perfect”? This saying is important. You must practice before going “live!” If you haven't practised enough, your audience will see the trick, and you don't want that.

Jasper Todd

GLOSSARY

Audience: People who watch a magic trick being performed.

Deck: A set of 52 playing cards (sometimes 54 if there are jokers).

Magic: A kind of art that involves performing a trick that makes impossible things happen.

Magician: A person who performs the magic.

Helper: A person who takes part in a certain activity like assisting a magician.

Perform: To carry out a certain act or action.

Shuffle: Sliding cards over each other to mix them up.

Trick: An act carried out by a magician that's meant to trick an audience.

(More detailed Glossary in Book 3 - the final book in the series of 'BIG MAGIC BOOKS FOR KIDS')

REFERENCES

Barnes, P. (2021, February 24). 15 Easy Card Tricks for Kids (2022 Guide). Mom Loves Best. https://momlovesbest.com/card-tricks-for-kids

A Guide to the Hindu Shuffle—Sleight of Hand Tutorials. (2016, September 23). The Illusionist's Foundation YouTube. https://www.youtube.com/watch?v=3xPwS43mWfg

How to Shuffle Cards for Beginners—Riffle Shuffle with Bridge in the Hands Tutorial. (2018, December 19). Jason Parker YouTube. https://www.youtube.com/watch?v=NdCia_d1u5c

How to SHUFFLE CARDS like a MAGICIAN (3 EASY TRICKS). (2020, March 28). Bao Magic YouTube. https://www.youtube.com/watch?v=RbknCzcVDEU

How to Shuffle Cards: The Hindu Shuffle. (2011, March 5). 52Kards YouTube. https://www.youtube.com/watch?v=ylifviUQHrI

LaScala, M. (2021, May 25). The 80 Best Jokes for Kids That Are Easy to Remember for a Quick Laugh. Good Housekeeping. https://www.goodhousekeeping.com/life/parenting/g28581033/best-jokes-for-kids/

Michelle. (2019, May 21). 8 Easy Card Tricks for Kids to Delight and Amaze. MyKidsTime. https://www.mykidstime.com/things-to-do/8-easy-card-tricks-for-kids-delight-amaze/

Ravi, A. (2020, November 5). 21 Easy Yet Amazing Magic Tricks With Cards For Kids. MomJunction. https://www.momjunction.com/articles/magic-tricks-with-cards-for-kids_00672206/#16-do-as-i-do-trick

16 Magic Jokes Fit For A Wizard. (2021, August 11). Beano. https://www.beano.com/posts/magic-jokes

MORE BOOKS BY JASPER TODD

Check out the next two books in the magic series for kids. We will dive deeper into self-working magic tricks, and tricks that use everyday objects.

Join us for the adventure! Collect them all!

Available on Amazon.

And if you've enjoyed this book then please leave us a review on Amazon.

We massively appreciate it.
Only takes a minute.

Thank you!

Made in the USA
Monee, IL
03 December 2023